Rosa M. Curto

Draw the Magic Fairy

Draw the Magic Pink Fairy

Enslow Elementary

an imprint of

Enslow Publishers, Inc.

40 Industrial Road
Box 398
Berkeley Heights, NJ 07922
USA

http://www.enslow.com

Colorful Candy

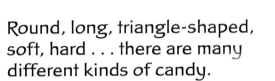

Round, long, triangle-shaped, soft, hard . . . there are many different kinds of candy.

Chocolates can come in different colors, too.

These are some of the candies that the pink fairy makes.

These lollipops are shaped like numbers!

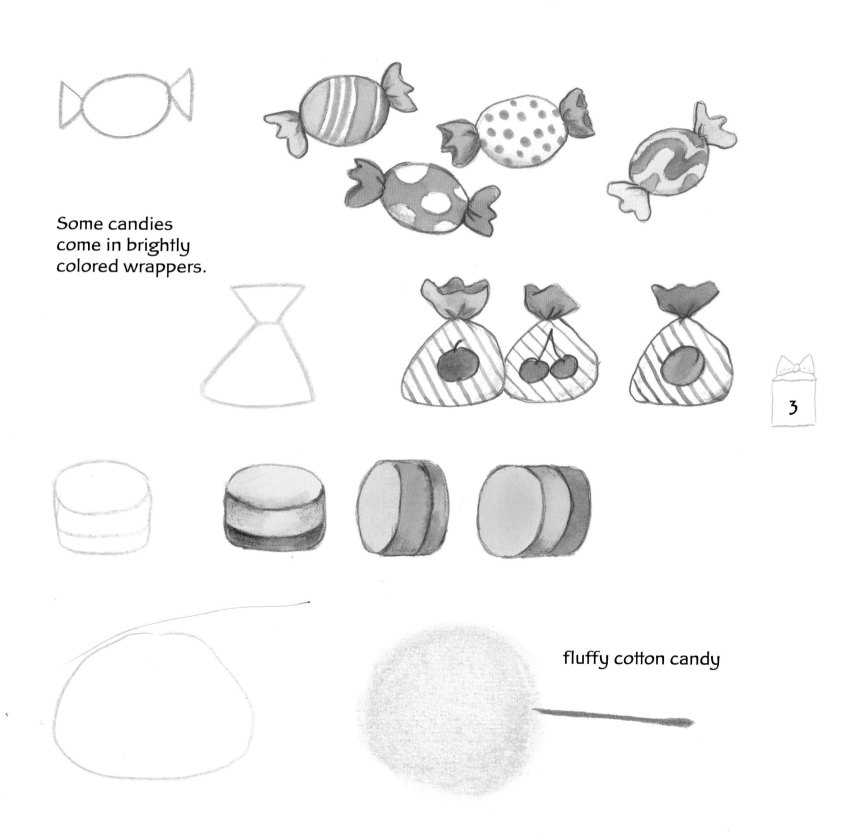

Some candies come in brightly colored wrappers.

fluffy cotton candy

3

Fancy Chocolates

The pink fairy and her friends enjoy
eating chocolates.

They love them so much!

4

At fairy parties, there are always pieces of fruit
covered in chocolate.

Try to draw some chocolates.
Create some new ones.

5

These shapes are very easy.
The second step is painting and decorating them.

A Bow for Every Occasion

The pink fairy makes bows that are many different shapes and colors.

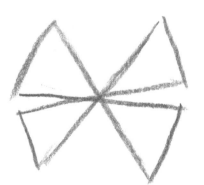

6

Fairies use bows for their hair and
their dresses. They also use them to decorate
for parties and to decorate their presents.

Presents With Love

8

It is very important to the fairies that their gifts
are perfectly wrapped.

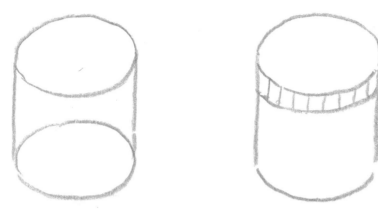

Giving pretty gifts is a way of showing love.

Now try this one in four steps!

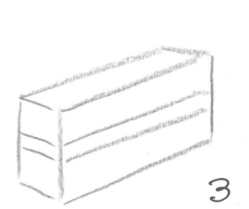

1

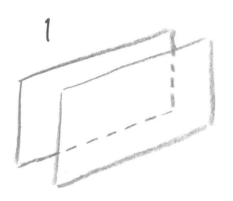

Draw two rectangles.

2

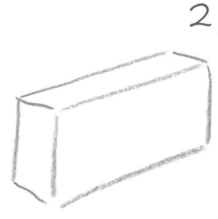

Connect three corners
to add volume.

Draw a ribbon.

3

9

The pink fairy loves
giving presents.

Add a bow!

4

Pretty Bottles and Boxes

The pink fairy has many small bottles.

10

If you want to make the pink fairy happy . . .

. . . give her a pretty bottle or a little decorated box!

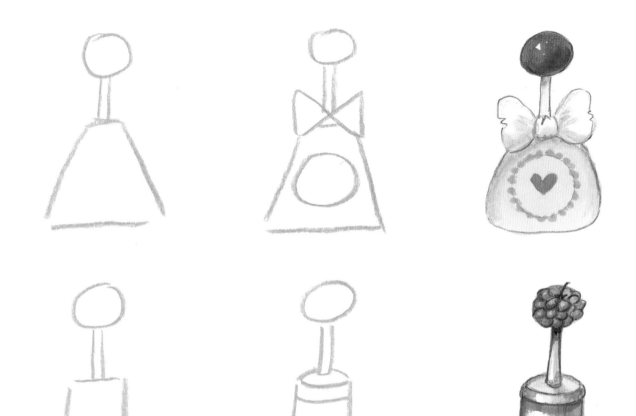

She uses them to store magic dust.

Accessories and Dresses

The pink fairy likes to go barefoot, but sometimes
she needs to protect her feet. She makes shoes from
leaves, petals, and smooth fruit skin.

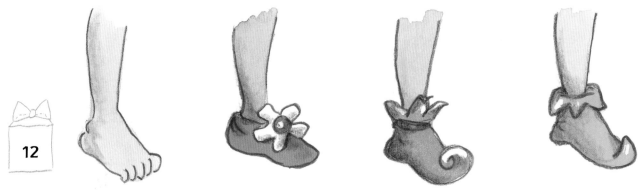

If you find a colored ribbon while walking through the forest,
it means that a fairy passed by there a short while ago!

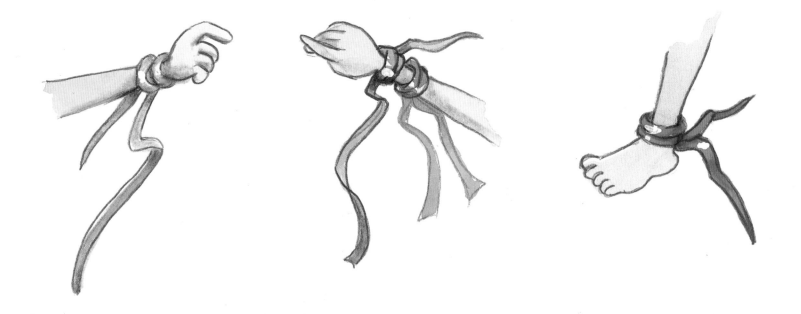

Both the fairies' dresses and their shoes smell nice.
They smell like the leaves and flowers they are made from.

Autumn dress

In autumn, fairies make their dresses from brown,
red, and yellow leaves that fall from the trees.

Spring dress

In spring, all the pretty flowers bloom. The fairies
can use green leaves and many colored petals for their dresses.

Flowers in the Fairy World

The fairy world would not exist without flowers. Fairies need flowers to make clothes, houses, and other important things. There would be no flowers without the fairies either. The fairies water and take care of the flowers.

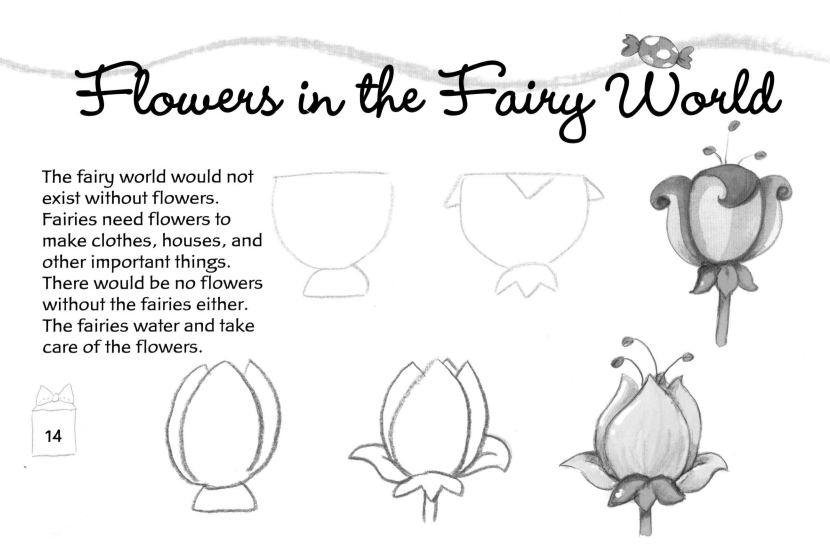

Some fairies like to make themselves small and hide inside the flowers that are still half-closed or bell-shaped. They can see everything from there. They like to watch what is going on around them.

You can draw a flower in three steps.

Look closely! This is the same flower in two different positions.

Look at the shapes carefully. Do not rush.
Drawing slowly will help you a lot.

Water Lilies

Water lilies are aquatic (uh-kwah-tik) plants.
This means that they live in water.

Their leaves float in still water.
Their flowers are full of petals and are very beautiful.

Undines (un-deens) are water fairies.
They live among the water lilies.

Draw a half-circle and a stem.

1

2

3

What about this one?

1

2

You can draw a beautiful flower in just four simple steps.

3

4

Fairies sit on water lilies to rest or sunbathe.

17

Sparkling Glowworms

Here are eight different glowworms you can draw in three steps.

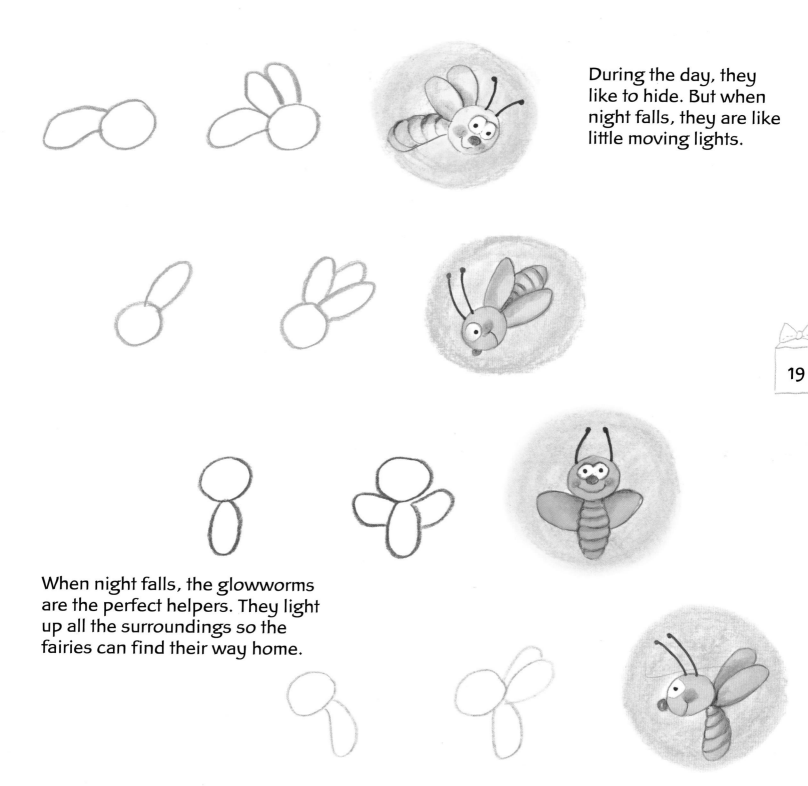

During the day, they like to hide. But when night falls, they are like little moving lights.

When night falls, the glowworms are the perfect helpers. They light up all the surroundings so the fairies can find their way home.

19

Tadpole and Frog

Draw a tadpole in four steps.

1

2

3

4

When the tadpole grows up, it becomes a frog.

1

Now draw a little frog. Start by joining two simple shapes together.

2

3

4

Draw the frog's feet and legs.

Paint it.

Would you like to draw another frog in five steps?

1 Draw two ovals.

2 Add the back legs.

Draw the eyes and front legs.

3

4

Round it off and paint it.

5

Frogs croak to talk to the water fairies. Frogs sing to let the fairies know when rain is coming.

Robbie the Raccoon

1

Draw two simple shapes.

2

Outline the arms.

3

Finish the arms.

22

4

Draw the ears, nose, and back legs.

5

23

Robbie is the magic pink fairy's favorite animal friend.

Finish the details.

6

Paint it!

The Pink Fairy

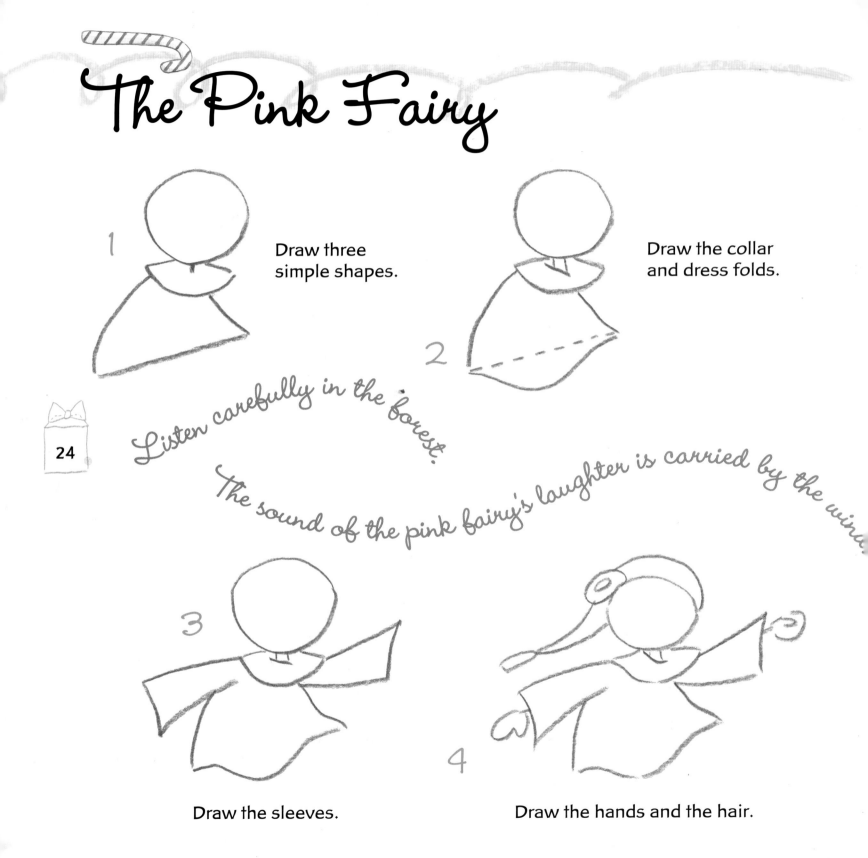

1   Draw three simple shapes.

2   Draw the collar and dress folds.

Listen carefully in the forest. The sound of the pink fairy's laughter is carried by the wind.

3   Draw the sleeves.

4   Draw the hands and the hair.

24

Outline the legs and the feet.

5

6

25

Draw the wings
and the braid.

7

Draw the face.
Finish the details and paint her.

The Mountain Fairy

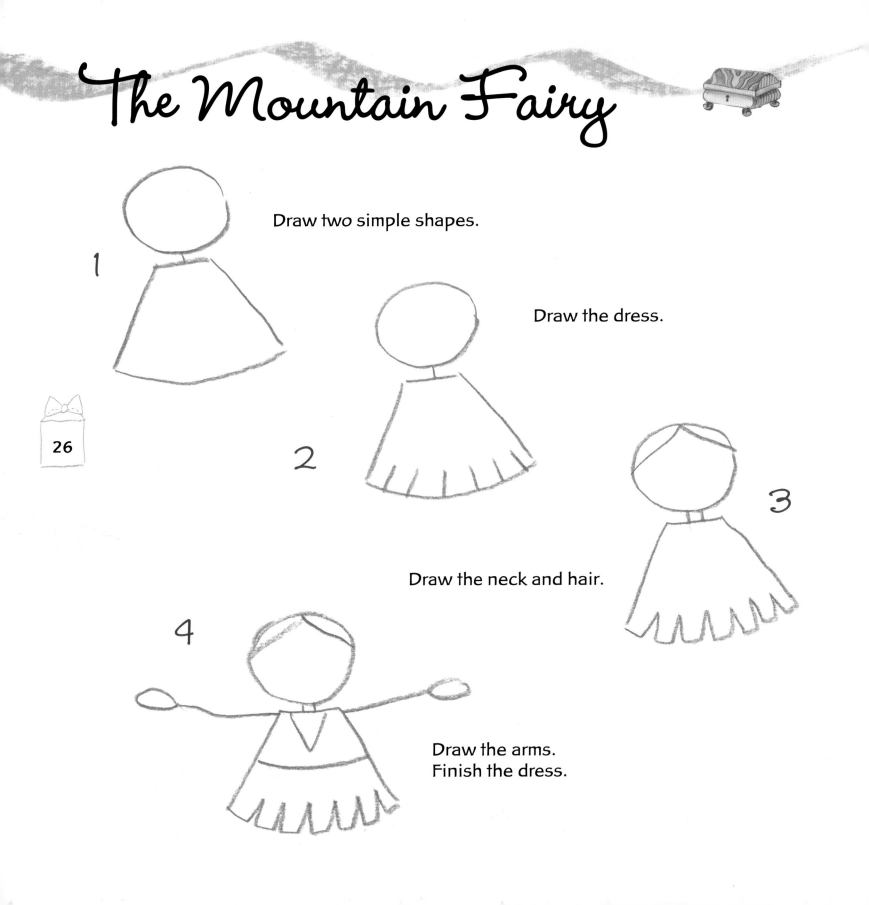

Draw two simple shapes.

1

Draw the dress.

2

26

Draw the neck and hair.

3

4

Draw the arms.
Finish the dress.

Draw the sleeves and the legs.

5

She is very wise and shares everything she knows.

6

Finish the legs and draw the wings.

Finish the details and paint her. The mountain fairy has gray hair, but she is young at heart.

7

27

Fairy Dana

28

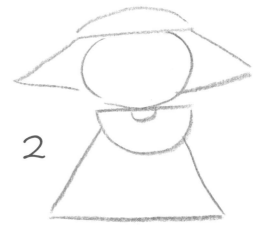

1 Draw three simple shapes.

2 Outline the hair and the neck.

3 Work on the hair and neck a bit more.

4 Add more details to the hair. Draw the dress and the ears.

5

Outline the arms and legs.

Finish the arms and the legs.

6

Draw the face and the wings. Finish the details and paint her.

7

Fairy Dana is the pink fairy's best friend.

29

Fairy Melissa

1 Draw a circle and a triangle.

2 Outline the arms.

30

3 Draw the legs.

4 Draw the dress with the sleeves.

Finish the hair, arms, and legs.

5

6

Draw the ears and the wings.

She is the best swimmer. She is a very happy fairy!

Finish the details and paint her.

7

Blending In

When fairies want to hide, they change how they look. They blend in with their surroundings. Some animals do this, too.

Fairies can change their color and shape.

They hide among the flowers,
leaves, trunks, clouds, and ears
of corn and wheat.

33

Now it is
time to draw!

Draw a fairy blending in with
her surroundings. Find the
names of animals that do
the same thing. For example,
one of these animals is the
polar bear. Their white fur lets them
blend into their snowy environment.

Imagine

Fairies use things from nature to make their houses. Their homes always smell very nice.

Can you see how the roof of this house was made? The mountain fairy used three leaves.

34

And how was this roof made? The pink fairy used a lovely flower.

Look!

How was this house drawn?

And this one?

Imagine a whole fairy village and draw it. Here is an example.

35

Enslow Elementary, an imprint of Enslow Publishers, Inc.
Enslow Elementary® is a registered trademark of Enslow Publishers, Inc.

Original title of the book in Catalan: *DIBUIXANT EL MÓN DE LES FADES 2*
Copyright © GEMSER PUBLICATIONS, S.L., 2012
C/ Castell, 38; Teià (08329) Barcelona, Spain (World Rights)
Tel: 93 540 13 53
E-mail: info@mercedesros.com
Web site: http://www.mercedesros.com
Author and illustrator: Rosa Maria Curto

Library of Congress Cataloging-in-Publication Data
Curto, Rosa Maria.
 [Dibuixant el món de les fades. 2. English]
 Draw the magic pink fairy / Rosa M. Curto.
    pages cm — (Draw the magic fairy)
 Summary: "Learn how to draw the world of the pink fairy, including her other fairy friends, different animals, food, flowers, clothes, and much more"—Provided by publisher.
  ISBN 978-0-7660-4266-7
 1. Drawing—Technique—Juvenile literature. 2. Fairies in art—Juvenile literature. I. Title.
 NC655.C87213 2013
 741.2—dc23

                         2012030436

Future edition:
Paperback ISBN 978-1-4644-0475-7

J
743.893
CUR

Printed in China
122012 Leo Paper Group, Heshan City, Guangdong, China
10 9 8 7 6 5 4 3 2 1